WALK

in the   **ince**

LLANDUDNO

The Dark Age Prince

Maelgwn Gwynedd

The Routes

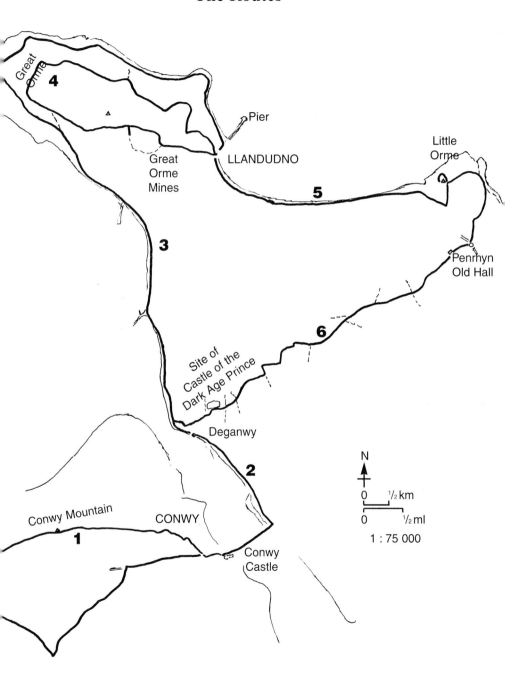

© Ralph Maddern

First published in Great Britain 2001

Focus Publications Ltd
58 Shelley Road
Stratford-upon-Avon
Warwickshire CV37 7JS

ISBN: 1-872050-09-3

Printed in Great Britain by
Lithographics of Worcester

Contents

Picture Illustration

Dave O'Shea - *Artistik Llanrwst*

Marine Archaeology

Nigel Bannerman

Centre of Power

as envisaged by

G W Cox

Llandudno and District Field Club 1910

Great Orme
Bronze Age Economy

Realm

of the

Dark Age Prince

When the Romans had departed from Britain, by the year 400, power was available to whoever could gather a band of warriors and hold ground against challengers. In North Wales, as elsewhere, some aspiring warlords would have served the Romans; some may have joined one of the many revolts against their rule that became increasingly frequent as the empire declined. During all that time an understanding could have been gained of what makes the exercise of power possible: possession of arms and determination to use them against those to be subjugated.

Contention between warlords continued after the Roman departure until, in various areas of Britain, there emerged chiefs to whom others could be forced or cajoled into offering allegiance. It was the legendary King Arthur who united indigenous British forces against Saxon invaders, scoring a decisive victory at Mount Badon about the year 518, by which time a warlord in North Wales, Caswallon, had established supremacy in this area against marauders from across the Irish and North Seas.

A century after the Roman departure almost all their literacy and learning had vanished, not least due to destructive activities by invading forces. Hence, there is a dire scarcity of records from which to derive knowledge of those times. A Dark Age implies an absence of these features. As Roman law had also disappeared, rulers could murder as an instrument of policy. When Caswallon died early in the sixth century his son, Maelgwn, murdered an uncle in order to establish himself as Prince of Gwynedd. It was not to be his last murder of a family member.

While relishing the role of an unscrupulous warrior and conqueror, Prince Maelgwn Gwynedd was influenced by the religious fervour of the times. This was also the age of the Dark Age Saints.

Llan

of a

Dark Age Saint

Saint Tudno, as he became known, was lucky. When hundreds of enthusiasts were travelling over sea and land, bringing the new enlightenment to whoever would give them time, Tudno alighted on that great mass of flinty limestone where copious springs flowed with a continuous supply of baptismal waters.

It was a rugged headland in the realm of that brutal warrior, Prince Maelgwn Gwynedd who preferred not to notice the new arrival. Tudno did not bear arms and seemed not to pose any kind of threat to the established power. If he did turn out to be an undesirable he could be easily cut down and his remains thrown over a cliff into the sea.

However, if truth were told, Maelgwn preferred to give any of these so-called saints who were going about the land a very wide berth. He feared no-one but felt nervous about the message they preached. They were setting up cells in all sorts of places and preaching the new gospel to anyone, anywhere, at any time. Also, some of his own bards had become disciples. Even his favourite, Taliesin, was an enthusiast.

If Maelgwn could not bring himself to call upon Tudno, he had a ready supply of spies who were always falling over themselves to do his bidding. He picked the brightest and sent him over to the headland. Tudno had set up a *Llan*, the spy reported. Everyone there was a disciple, even the cave dwellers at the bottom of the cliffs. More astounding was the change in the spy himself: he returned spouting Tudno's message, and even tried to convert the courtiers. Of course, the bards were the keenest listeners.

Maelgwn felt uneasy. To regain the initiative he must do something spectacular. Just now there were no battles to fight, no enemies to subdue. As he pondered his eye settled on that summit across the estuary. He grinned maliciously and summoned his bards and musicians. They must face a severe test, he told them; and he would see who was best.

Route 1

To tread the ground of the Dark Age Prince as a patron of the arts find the centre of Conwy.

Conwy - Conwy Mountain - Sychnant Pass - Conwy: 8.8km, 5.5ml.

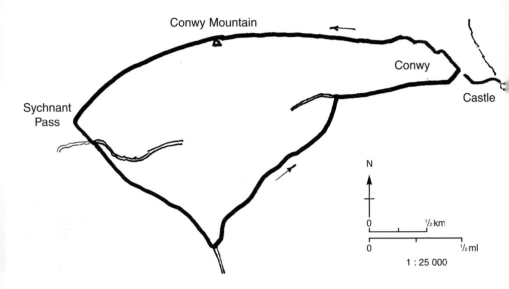

From Lancaster Square walk NW beneath the town wall arch and along the main road, turn left across the bridge spanning the railway (0.3km) and right along Cadnant Park Road which veers left to Mountain Road (0.6km).

At 0.8km turn right from Mountain Road up to the ridge and continue westward above the estuary and the sea to the summit (2.5km, 1.6ml; elevation 246m, 809ft).

Imagine a timespan backwards of almost 1500 years. A band of weary musicians carry their sodden instruments up from the river and along the ridge. On the summit stone sits the Dark Age Prince laughing gleefully at their discomfort. Around him is gathered a circle of 24 court bards enjoying their chief's favour. Unencumbered by instruments these bards had swum the river at their Prince's command and were now in good fettle to present their verses which they had prepared in the place now known as the Vardre, the site of Deganwy Castle.

The Prince, deciding suddenly on doing something spectacular, had commanded his bards and musicians to swim to the farther shore and assemble on this height for a competition which he would judge. There may have been an element of fear in his impulse, for among his bardic circle was one whose thrust could be more deadly than that of a sword or spear. His name was Taliesin. He had a curious way of speaking his mind to the Prince through exquisitely barbed poetic lines. Maelgwn felt he would like to break free of Taliesin's influence but somehow he could not.

The competition had, of course, been fixed in advance by the cunning Prince in favour of his own bards. The year might have been 540. The event is marked as the first eisteddfod.

*   *   *

Descend from this aerial viewpoint - encompassing Puffin Island, Anglesey (NW), the Great Orme (N), Llandudno 030°, Deganwy 060°, Tywyn 080°, Llandudno Junction 100°, Conwy Castle 105°, Glan Conwy 120°, Upper Conwy Valley 180°. Now cast an eye back to Anglesey - Ynys Môn - where Caswallon, Maelgwn's father, won a crucial battle - *Brwydr Cerrig y Gwyddyl* - The Battle of the Stones of the Irish - by devising an unusual method to ensure his soldiers would face the enemy. He tied their horses' tails together. Unable to turn and flee, it was victory or death. They defeated a large army of Irish invaders, secured the island for Gwynedd and continuation of its ruling dynasty for 300 years.

*   *   *

Continue W/SW to Sychnant Pass (4.3km, 2.7ml; elevation: 122m, 400 ft). *Sych* means dry, *nant* is a gorge. *Sychnant:* dry gorge.

Cross the road and follow the path SE to the cottage *Pen- y-bwlch -* top of the pass - and on down to a council road (5.8km, 3.6ml). Continue SE along the road for about 100m, turn left (NE) through two critch-cratches by a cottage to critch-cratch 3, N to a fence gate (6.1km) and NE, passing *Coed Hendre* - Hendre Wood - on the right, to critch- cratch 4 (6.6km, 4.1ml). Turn right and follow the drive E through Oakwood Park to a council road. Cross the road to critch-cratch 5 and continue NE to critch-cratch 6, turn left and bear N over a stile to critch-cratch 7 by the council road (7.6km, 4.8ml). Turn right and continue E along the road to Conwy.

Look at the rock Conwy Castle stands on. It provides the foundation of a fortress built in the 1280s by King Edward the First to consolidate English power. Possession of this strategic bastion, with its medieval-type town walls built at the same time as the castle, gave the conqueror and his dynasty significant advantage over the whole area of North Wales for the next 350 years, especially during periods of rebellion and civil war. Treasures that were present in the fortress town include:

Aberconwy House (15thC), on the corner of Castle
and High Streets

Plas-mawr (1576-95), in High Street

22 High Street (16thC)

Parlwr-mawr (late 16thC), on the north side of Chapel Street

Old College House (early 16thC), on the west side of Castle Street

Plas-coch (16thC), Lancaster Square

11 Castle Street (1589).

That era passed with the end of the Civil War in the mid-17th century. Then minds turned to the possibility of using Conwy as a strategic location of a different kind - to provide a transport link between nations.

When the Dark Age Prince ruled Gwynedd the centre of power was on the eastern side of the river where the Prince had his court. That castle has vanished leaving nothing but the two hills on which it stood.

Imagination can assign the same fate to Conwy Castle which is only half the age of Prince Maelgwn's castle - had it survived to the present. Think of the noble rock which guards the entrance to the Conwy River as if a geological eruption had placed it there.

* * *

Route 2

Conwy Castle - Deganwy Castle (The Vardre): 4.3km, 2.7ml

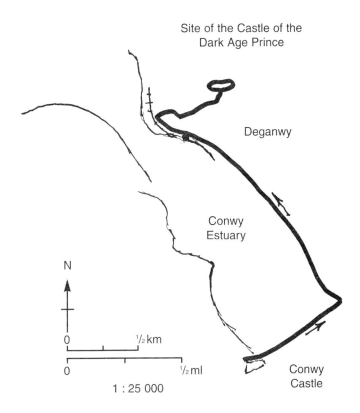

Site of the Castle of the
Dark Age Prince

Deganwy

Conwy
Estuary

N

0   ½ km

0   ½ ml

1 : 25 000

Conwy
Castle

From the Rock of Conwy (Conwy Castle) set out eastward across the river. Historically, this is one of the most significant estuary crossings in the world. The defending Welsh relied on its hazards. The Romans would not attempt it: they aimed their invasion upstream at Caerhun (Canovium) which provided a strategic base from which to march westward across the mountains to the Straits. The Normans took 200 years to establish their fortress base on the western shore, which, in the following centuries, left this vital jugular in the capricious hands of ferrymen who relished their power. Could England and Ireland communicate via this treacherous water? A suspension road bridge was constructed in 1826. Then the great railway engineer, Robert Stephenson, clinched the matter. The first Irish Mail train went through on 1st August 1848, taking with it Greenwich Mean Time to all station clocks.

Turn down steps (1.0km) from the bridge, then left to Deganwy Quay (2.8km).

All about looks permanent, as if everything has been in place since the beginning of time. We may now undermine the evidence of our eyes.

Climate is ever changing, adjusting to the earth's condition and forces acting upon it in the surrounding universe. A river reflects these changes in its physical features.

Go out onto the estuary sands at low tide and wander where forests grew. Look carefully at a dark object protruding through the sand and you may find evidence of wood thousands of years old. This is a vast plain that shrinks the southern mountains to insignificance, matching only with a sky arching from the horizon.

Rocks tell an even more ancient tale. There are pieces of hard mountain from around Penmaenmawr that provided tools for Stone Age Europeans. Examine a different texture and one may find a stranger from Scotland stranded far from home when an icy pusher from the north met a stoical thrust from a Welsh glacier.

Here is land that the sea has claimed by relentless encroachment and erosion.

Nigel Bannerman, marine archaeologist, has prepared the map on page 19 which suggests the estuary's contours at the time of the Dark Age Prince when sea level could have been up to two metres - about six and a half feet - lower than now.

Legend

——————————— HW coastline in 500

—·——·——·—· LW coastline in 500

=============== Trackways in 500

Conwy Bay in the Sixth Century

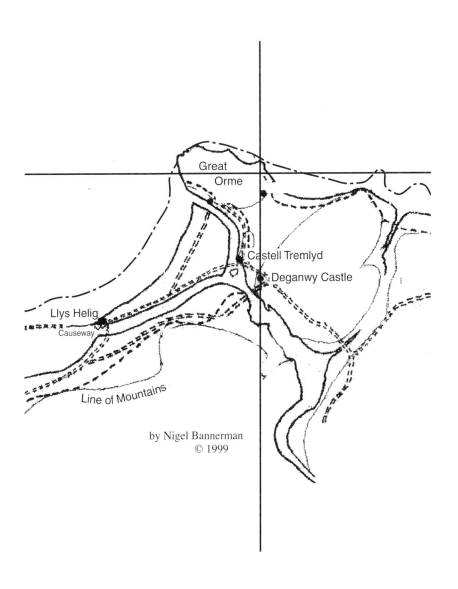

by Nigel Bannerman
© 1999

Deganwy Castle, Restored.

G. W. Cox, del.

Continue to the Deganwy train station (3.2km). At 3.5km, turn right along York Road to a path and left to a critch-cratch (3.9km).

Enter another world, one not unlike the environs of the Dark Age Prince's court in its own time. Here on the landscape are twelve mounds which could have served as useful lookout posts. Climb the mound nearest the shore and imagine the bay as it could have been in Maelgwn Gwynedd's time when the shoreline was out where the map indicates, and vegetation covered land now submerged.

Go towards a block of masonry marking the position of a gatehouse at the entrance to the castle. Continue left up a pathway leading to the summit and the centre of Maelgwn's Court (4.3km, 2.7m1).

Are we in a place of seminal beginning of Welsh culture? Across the water is Conwy Mountain, where Prince Maelgwn is said to have hosted the first eisteddfod. The same Maelgwn who, having fancied his nephew's wife, murdered his own wife, murdered the nephew and ravaged the murdered man's wife. It was all done in the same night, so a chronicler wrote.

Only Taliesin could curb the ruthless Prince's passions, which may confirm the might of pen over sword; for while the bard's lines endure, nothing of Maelgwn remains. His castle crumbled. Six centuries later the Normans recognised the advantage of this site and raised a castle of their own. The accompanying illustrations by G W Cox, published by G A Humphries in 1910, depict one of their constructions.

Follow the Dark Age Prince round the terrain of the castle on page 22: from gatehouse F on the plan, up the slope to gatehouse H, around the motte into the bailey M, down to the rear entrance P, into chapel Q, down to exit B and around the second motte to entrance A.

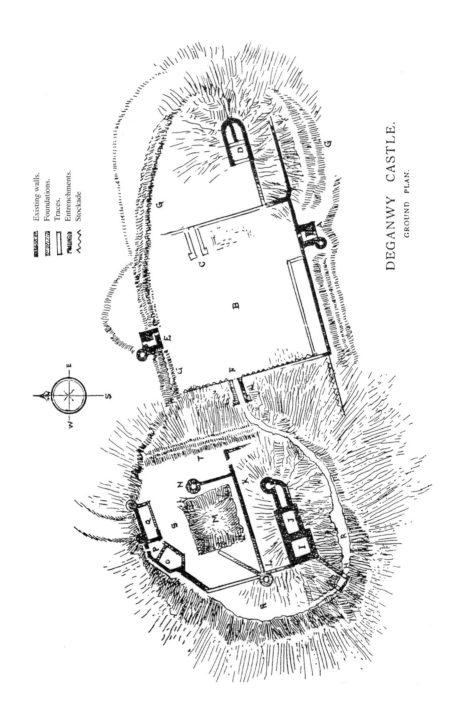

DEGANWY CASTLE.

GROUND PLAN.

Existing walls.
Foundations.
Traces.
Entrenchments.
Stockade

Route 3

Deganwy train station - round the Great Orme - Pen-trwyn Bronze Age smelting site - Llandudno: 13.2km, 8.3ml.

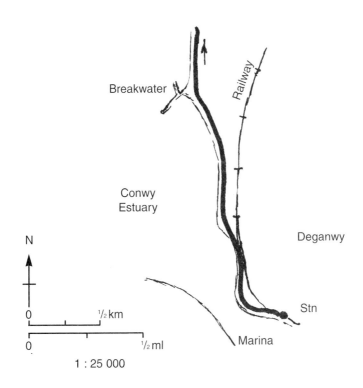

Northward from the train station veer left across the railway line and continue along the coast path to the breakwater, also known as Black Rocks (2.3km, 1.4ml).

The sea hides the secrets of ages, some of which have been revealed by research associated with the *Bronze Age Coast Project* (Nigel Bannerman, 2000).

Here was a fort known as Castell Tremlyd. If the Romans established it - sea level then could have been about two metres lower than now - the Dark Age Prince used it as a tideline outpost. In later centuries a thriving fishing community developed around the fort. It was known as Penlassoc. A ferry linked the settlement with the opposite shore.

CASTELL TREMLYD

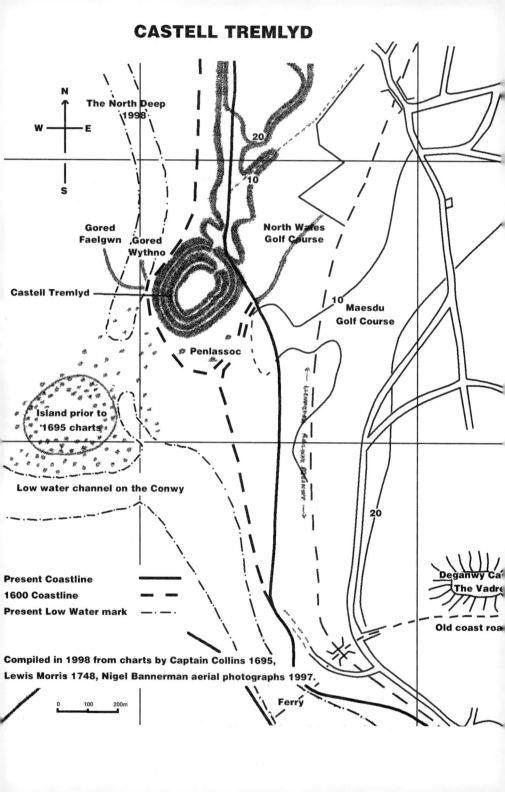

N
↑
W ← + → E
↓
S

The North Deep
1998

20

10

Gored
Faelgwn   Gored
Wythno

North Wales
Golf Course

Castell Tremlyd

10

Maesdu
Golf Course

Penlassoc

Island prior to
1695 charts

Low water channel on the Conwy

20

Deganwy Ca
The Vadre

Old coast roa

Present Coastline ———
1600 Coastline – – –
Present Low Water mark —·—·

Compiled in 1998 from charts by Captain Collins 1695,
Lewis Morris 1748, Nigel Bannerman aerial photographs 1997.

0   100   200m

Ferry

Nigel Bannerman's map on page 24 suggests how it was about 1600, with fish-trap structures at the foot of the fort embankment. Gored Faelgwn - Maelgwn's weir - and Gored Wythno, could provide a regular supply of protein for communities on shore. No boats were needed, only servicing to keep the weir - made of timber fencing supported by boulders - intact and free from weeds.

Most of the inhabitants of Tremlyd and Penlassoc were wiped out in the Black Death plague which reached its most severe phase in 1349. Those who survived would have been joined in due course by incomers. A lengthy revival process followed. By 1532 there was again an active community here at Tremlyd and Penlassoc. In that year the Crown granted ferrying rights to residents Edward and Elizabeth Weldon, as well as other privileges which were vigorously contested from within the community. The dispute was sufficiently contentious to be referred for resolution to the Star Chamber in London.

Fish traps were so effective in supplying sustenance that rulers were quick to seize control, allowing their subjects access only under licence. The Tremlyd fish traps and others could have provided Deganwy Castle with a regular supply of fresh sea food for Prince Maelgwn's court.

*　*　*

A sighting line approximately west-south-west from Tremlyd will lie above a legendary palace known as Llys Helig ap Glannawg. It is marked on the sixth-century map of Conwy Bay - page 19. A story of how the palace and its inhabitants were inundated and submerged beneath the sea is told in Tom Parry's work, Llys Helig (1996). Also included is a description of various expeditions organised during two centuries to survey Llys Helig's exact location and dimensions.

*　*　*

How would the Dark Age Prince have responded to the rising sea swallowing his near neighbour, Helig ap Glannawg, who held a low-lying part of the kingdom? Perhaps with less than special notice: Helig was, after all, a mere subject, while Maelgwn styled himself variously as King of Gwynedd, King of Wales, and - as successor to the legendary King Arthur - King of Britain. Such a man of eminence was he.

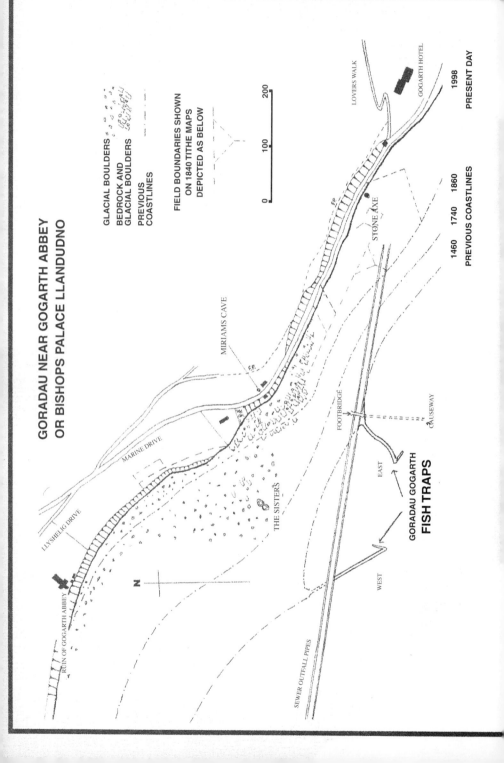

GORADAU NEAR GOGARTH ABBEY OR BISHOPS PALACE LLANDUDNO

GLACIAL BOULDERS
BEDROCK AND GLACIAL BOULDERS
PREVIOUS COASTLINES

FIELD BOUNDARIES SHOWN ON 1840 TITHE MAPS DEPICTED AS BELOW

0   100   200

PRESENT DAY

1998

1460   1740   1860

PREVIOUS COASTLINES

GOGARTH HOTEL

LOVERS WALK

STONE AXE

MIRIAMS CAVE

F.P.

F.P.

MARINE DRIVE

LLYSHELIG DRIVE

RUIN OF GOGARTH ABBEY

THE SISTERS

N

SEWER OUTFALL PIPES

FOOTBRIDGE

CAUSEWAY

EAST

WEST

GORADAU GOGARTH
FISH TRAPS

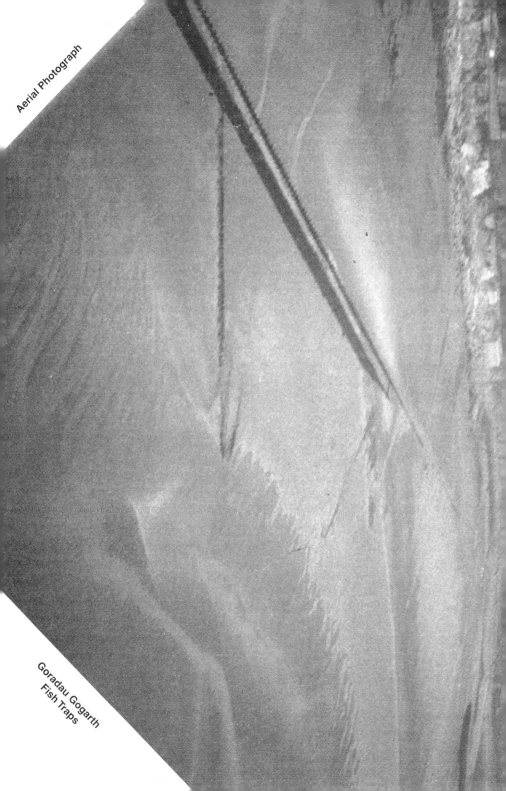

Aerial Photograph

Goradau Gogarth
Fish Traps

And he would have been well aware that tragedy for some can bring benefit for others. A higher sea level could offer improved self-defence, and possibly provide more abundant harvests from the sea which could be gathered most effectively by the the use of fish traps, most conveniently at the foot of Castell Tremlyd. He would, of course, ensure the weirs were strictly under his personal command, with his own name upon them, so as to make it clearly understood there would be swift retribution for any poachers.

*　*　*

Treading the coast path northward, which leads to the marine drive, we arrive above the site of a Bishop's Palace - that of the Bishop of Bangor - also known as Gogarth Abbey. Monks retreated here in the 13th century. It was a remote location, very suitable for meditation, contemplation and prayer, an activity that could only become viable if a ready supply of food and drink could be ensured. There were trustworthy examples to follow.

One was the Dark Age St Tudno who, six centuries earlier, had identified the Great Orme's fresh water springs and thereby founded the modern town and resort. The other was the Dark Age Prince Maelgwn who established a reliable economic base for his regime by building handy fish traps, most conveniently near the lower fort of Tremlyd.

The monks, being practical men, erected their fish traps so they were readily accessible at low tide when trapped fish could be easily gathered. Of course, sea levels were lower when the monks were in residence. The illustration on page 26 published by Diane and Nigel Bannerman in their work *The Great Orme Explained 2001* suggests sea levels in 1860, 1740 and 1460. The monks' fish traps are shown with the 19th century sewer pipe built across them.

On page 27 a reproduced aerial photograph from the Bannermans' publication displays what is visible of the Gogarth fish traps at very low tides.

As in the time of the Dark Age Prince, State Authority could not resist taking intrusive interest in fish traps. In the 1860s an Act of Parliament declared fish traps to be illegal and required them to be dismantled. Fortunately, "the rows of stones that helped form the fish weirs and supported the posts and wattle did not have to be completely scattered, for these are what still remain ..." Nigel Bannerman: *The Bronze Age Coast Project.*

* * *

Beyond the Orme's Head (8.1km, 5ml) the N/NE coast is usually more sheltered than the west side, an advantage earlier inhabitants put to commercial use.

In Britain the period of time known as The Bronze Age extended from 4,300 to 2,500 years ago. It was a period of special significance here on the Great Orme where copper, one of the two metals used to make bronze, is known to have been mined from about 3,860 to 2,600 years ago. Copper ore was brought from a mine inland to the headland, Pen-trwyn (11.2km, 7ml).

"This site represents the earliest evidence for copper smelting yet discovered in Great Britain."
(Gwynedd Archeological Trust, March 1999)

This was a convenient place for treating the mined copper ore. After smelting, the molten copper metal would have been shaped into moulds of suitable size to be loaded as cargo in an ocean-going boat which was docked at the bottom of the cliff. This was the only good sea access available on the Great Orme.

With a cargo of copper metal loaded, Bronze Age mariners would push the boat out and head off.

Where did they go? Perhaps to Cornwall. The south-west peninsula was the only area of Britain where tin as well as copper was mined. Or, they may have gone south on a trading mission along the Atlantic coast to the Mediterranean. What did they bring back on the return voyage? Research is underway seeking answers to these and other intriguing questions.

* * *

Bronze Age kiln

Bronze Age Boat →

A Saint's Town

in a

Prince's Realm

Southward along the marine drive is the town of the Dark Age Saint (13.2km, 8.3ml).

A town which can wear many labels, including: internationally known resort; distinguished conference destination; queen of the west. It was once a settlement on the Great Orme of round cells resembling beehives.

What a shock would overcome the sixth-century Saint - if he were to turn up among the tourists.

The Dark Age Prince would also gaze in disbelief. Not only would the Saint and the Prince mutter incredulities at the transformation. But look! This marshy shingle bar, prone to flooding in rough weather, was scarcely worth a second glance if you were not ready to build a fish trap.

Could this really be St Tudno's Llan?

The Prince's mind would turn to the plentiful stocks of game in the woods to the south; the Saint would think of the unending flow of fresh spring water just up there, up on the headland. Had the springs stopped flowing, causing the inhabitants to migrate? He would be impatient to find out.

Route 4

Llandudno - St Tudno's Church - Great Orme Copper Mines - Llandudno: 9.0km, 5.6ml.

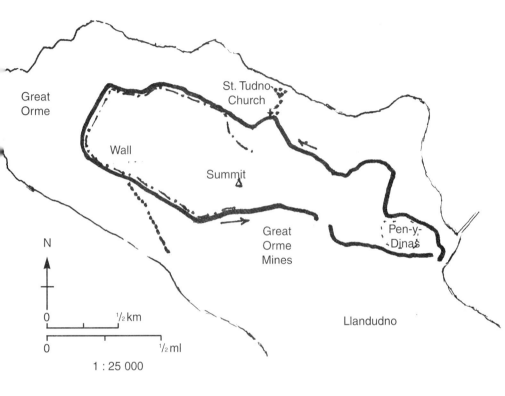

On the trail of the Dark Age Saint,
And keen-eyed copper prospectors,
Retrace millennia distant,
And discover ancient actors.

From the pier entrance veer left at 0.2km and again at 0.4km, across the Happy Valley park to steps leading around the northern base of Pen y Dinas. At the top of the Pen one may imagine the date is 1,000 BC, the beginning of the later Bronze Age, when settled mining and pastoral communities felt concern about invaders pushing in from distant lands. Of course, the locals were themselves descendants of invaders who had arrived here to mine copper. That time had now been all but forgotten. The real worry was that these new invaders had been reported as being well armed and ruthless warriors: a formidable threat to folk who had allowed their combat skills to lapse in favour of developing mining techniques.

From this hill, lookouts could have a long view to the east, south and west, and give their communities advance warning of approaching enemies.

Continue to a critch-cratch (1.2km) behind the Ski Lodge, northward to a crest and sea view (1.4km), NW veering to W with the Orme summit directly ahead, to a critch-cratch alongside Pink Farm (2.0km). Beyond the farmhouse and a critch-cratch, discover the area of assured fresh water supply that the Dark Age Saint sought to support his base and mission. St Tudno's instinct and sharp observation enabled him to locate the springs which have continued an uninterrupted flow since the day he arrived. Until the late nineteenth century these wells were essential contributors to Llandudno's water supply.

From Ffynnon Powell (2.5km), continue through the next critch-cratch to St Tudno's Church, the assumed site of a cell which the sixth-century crusader established here. The cell may have been simply a circular dry stone wall thatched with branches and any kind of vegetation. Other cells, some of wattle and mud, would have been built around St Tudno's as the Saint attracted disciples. Thus the first Llan - Tudno, the church and settlement of Tudno, which mutated easily to Llan - dudno - appeared on this landscape.

Very soon the Saint acquired a seaside residence - setting a precedent for the resort that would evolve in the following millennium. He is said to have occupied Ogof Llech, the seashore cave where he retreated for meditation and relaxation.

This was another piece of luck for St Tudno, for he had alighted on this mass of flinty limestone where weather and time had fashioned several wondrous caves which had been occupied during the Stone and Bronze Ages for several thousands of years. So, the Dark Age Saint was a very late arrival. But he had one advantage over all his predecessors: he could preach a fantastic message.

Oh, could he preach! - such incredible revelations brought him instant success amongst cave dwellers who had never heard the like. Not only did they become his devoted disciples; they begged him to join their own community. The choice of cave would be entirely his own. The properties available to the Saint we now know as: Hiding Cave - Ogof Llech; Hornby Cave; Ogof Hafnant; Ogof Colomenod - Pigeons Cave; Dutchman's Cave; Kendrick's Cave. All have fascinating stories attached to their names, the most interesting being the longevity of human tenure - from about 12,000 years ago, following glaciation withdrawal. Even in later times the caves have been occasionally occupied.

A zig-zag path from the Llan, now embedded in the hillside, provided access between the caves and the Llan.

Up the cliff where baptismal waters flowed in the tiny settlement of Llandudno, a church arose which served as the parish spiritual centre until 1839 when a storm ripped its roof off; leaving it derelict until 1855 when it was restored. But by then the engines of economics had run over St Tudno's concept. His 'Llan' - Llandudno - had rearranged itself on the neck of land down by the sea shore, leaving its source of original inspiration isolated here.

*   *   *

Continue westward along the cemetery boundary, southward then NW (3.1km) along a farm track to a gate (3.8km) and a track intersection. Follow the stone wall to the northern corner, turn south-west and encounter, on the right, a curious feature: The Swallit Hole, which may have been formed in glacial times as a drainage sump.

Further along are the remains of a large stone circle; nearby is a hut circle.

Marking the western wall corner (4.6km) is a cairn which may have been established as a Neolithic symbol and continues to receive contributions.

Continue south-eastward above an expanding view of aerial seascape 290 to 340 degrees - to the southern wall corner (6.4km, 4.0ml), and eastward (080 degrees) to the copper heart of the Great Orme (7.2km, 4.5 ml).

*   *   *

A site of immense antiquity. An incredible example of primary metal production over periods totalling about 1,350 years.

The Great Orme Mines "will probably re-shape our knowledge of the commercial history of the Bronze Age." (Simon Walker, International Mining Magazine)

Here was "probably the largest copper mine in antiquity." (Mark Randall, University College, London)

Radiocarbon dating has established that copper was mined here for 1,260 years from 1860 BC to 600 BC. After a lapse of 1,300 years, copper mining was resumed in 1692 and continued intermittently until 1881.

In 1987 the site was due to become a car park when a feasibility study revealed the significance of what was here.

Bronze Age mining began with a selection of stones on the beaches. Hard stones were required, suitable for use as hammers.

"Over 2,500 stone hammers have been found ranging in size from 4 to 64 pounds 2 to 29 kilos," the company states. "Almost all of these would have been hand held, but a few show signs that they may have had handles fitted. The job of selecting stones may have been a profession in its own right."

Pestle and Mortar:
preparing copper ore for smelting
with hand-held pounder

Raw hide binds handle to stone hammer

Impressions in the stone head
secures the handle

Long handle: powerful force

Bone tools were used to scrape away broken rock

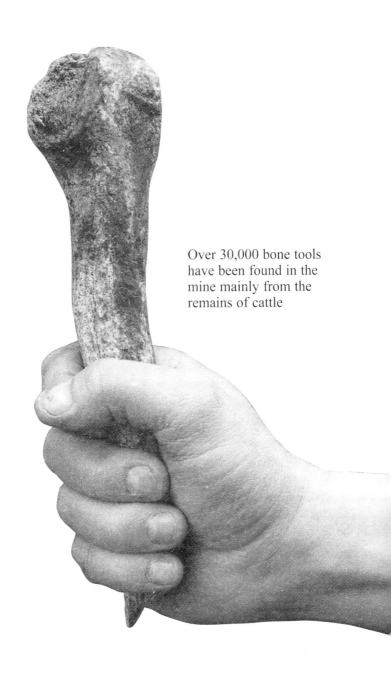

Over 30,000 bone tools
have been found in the
mine mainly from the
remains of cattle

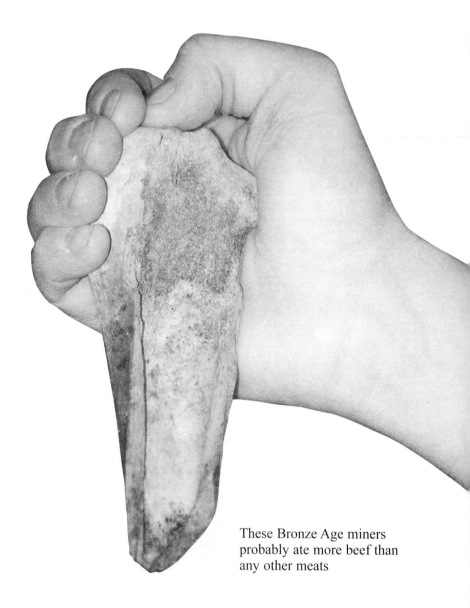

These Bronze Age miners
probably ate more beef than
any other meats

These bone tools may have lain underground for about 3,000 years

If the miners struck a section of rock too hard for stone and bone tools, a fire was lit against it. On cooling, the rock would contract and become easier to break.

"Evidence of firesetting has been found at a depth of 220 feet below the surface, which suggests a sophisticated system of ventilation must have been in place."

Broken rock containing copper ore was carried to the surface where waste rock was separated by crushing and then washing with water. The remaining copper ore could have been conveyed to a smelting site such as at Pen-trwyn headland and placed in a clay kiln.

The kiln temperature was raised to 1,100 degrees centigrade using charcoal as a fuel and subjecting it to a current of air pumped from a leather bellows.

The molten metal was poured into moulds of suitable shape and size for export as cargo in an ocean-going boat docked at the bottom of the Pen-trwyn cliff. As unalloyed copper metal is too soft to use for tools or weapons a source of tin had to be found for production of bronze.

Tin had been mined on the moorlands of south-west Britain - from Devon through to West Cornwall - for at least as long as the copper deposits on the Great Orme had been worked. However, as copper was also mined on the south-west peninsula it seems probable that Great Orme mariners traded their copper for tin and returned with a cargo to forge bronze.

Research is being undertaken to piece together the fragments of these complex stories that will shed light on the history of this land and its inhabitants.

*　*　*

Bronze Age folk lived here, burrowing in the earth to extract copper ore, for more than 1,200 years. Over that time they may have reproduced through about 50 generations. How did they manage a self-sufficiency in isolation?

An expanse of grass, mainly on the upper headland, provided lush pasture for their cattle and other grazing animals. Along the beaches, women and children could gather harvests from fish traps, as well as mussels, cockles and other sea creatures. Some of the men were experienced seafarers, entirely familiar with waters around the headland. They could also use their ocean-going craft for deep-sea fishing.

All this was possible because the headland provided a continuous supply of fresh spring water which the Dark Age Saint discovered a thousand years after the last generation of Bronze Age copper miners had abandoned their homes.

Those homes - comprised a circular stone base supporting rafters rising to a conical apex and covered with thatch. They could have been spaced around the headland and along the isthmus in random pattern not dissimilar to the way mining communities appeared on landscapes across the world wherever discoveries of copper, gold, silver and other metals drew a rush of hopeful prospectors.

But in contrast to the rapid transition from boom settlement to ghost town, which has been a familiar feature of mining discoveries followed by exhaustion of supply in recent centuries, this community lasted about as long as ancient Greece.

During the passage of generations, curiosities about their origins would have been a subject of conversation in the conical huts. Where had they come from? the young would have asked. How had they arrived here? Older storytellers might relate as best they could tales told by forebears extending back into distant time. Myth and legend had to fill gaps and eventually there would have developed a whole canon of experience depicting the community's reflection of itself.

This aspect of cultural development could have flourished during the middle period when the community was settled and relatively undisturbed.

Later, a wave of invaders could have caused disturbance to the settled life. As warriors in search of metal for weapons the new arrivals offered a market to a mining community with centuries of experience in copper and bronze production. Mutual and self-interest could have been the deciding factor between invaders and invaded. This facilitated trade enabling the mining community to continue until that irresistible force, technological obsolescence, sounded an ominous message.

Newcomers brought the startling revelation that a stronger metal - iron - was in the market and increasingly sought by warriors and craftsmen.

Copper was still available in these tunnels, as 18th- and 19th~entury miners were to prove.

There may have been a long period of indecision and a piecemeal drifting away.

Eventually, that double-act of inevitability, supply and demand, drew down a stage curtain.

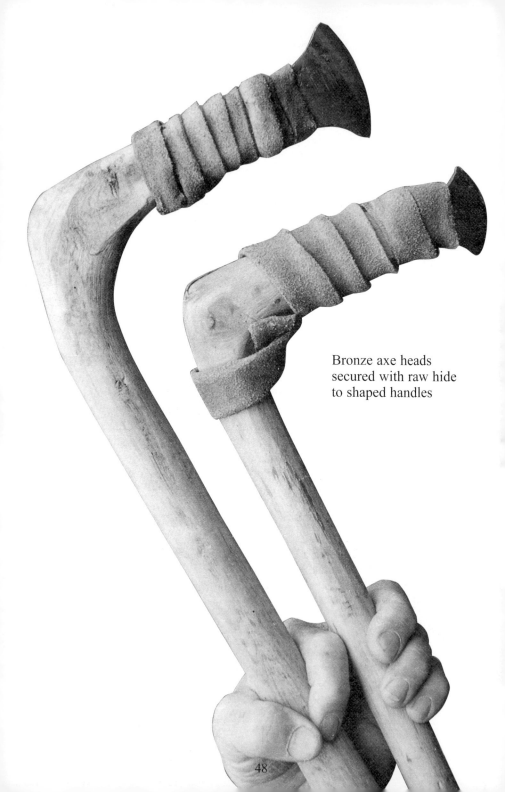

Bronze axe heads
secured with raw hide
to shaped handles

48

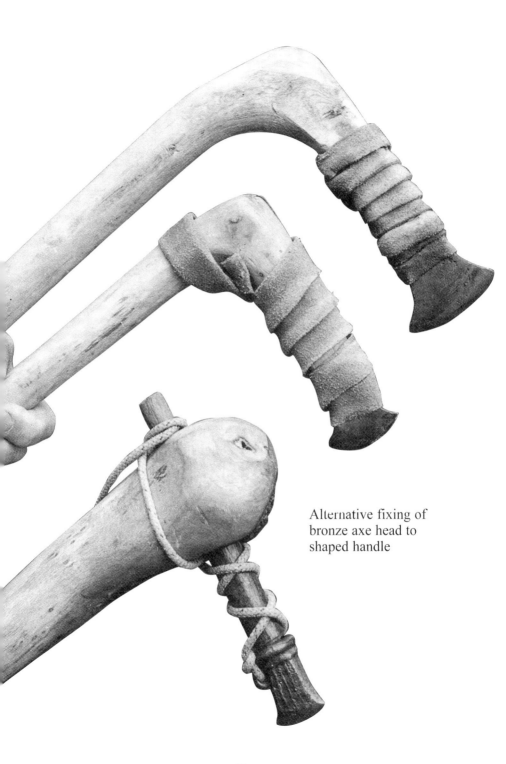

Alternative fixing of
bronze axe head to
shaped handle

St Tudno's Town

Descending from his sixth-Century Llan of beehive cells to this breathtaking sight would pressure his acute imagination into quick adjustment.

With flexible understanding the Dark Age Saint might ask if this could represent an extension of his own concept. Here the world comes to relax, reflect and recharge. And some of the world seeks to probe, proselytise and proclaim - just as he was apt to do up there on the headland.

Therefore, he could accept the transfiguration. Being a man who liked to probe deep into souls, he would need to go about in search of inner meanings and origins. In a word he would be on a trek after truth.
He may not have been aware of the Chinese philosopher's proverb:

To forget one's ancestors is to be a brook without a source,
a tree without roots

but his sentiments would surely chime with it.

He would discover that the richness of St Tudno's Town lies most profoundly in the will of its publicists - equivalent to his disciples - to seek out every source and explore every root.   The chroniclers began very early in the migration from St Tudno's Llan to this isthmus. If the second beginning - after St Tudno's on the headland - is set at 1849, the first trickle in what was to become a guidebook cascade appeared in 1835.

Bibliophile David Atkinson has identified 30 guidebooks to Llandudno published between 1850 and 1877. The flow continues, as does the inspiration and energy in search of sources and roots - a discovery that would warm the Saint's heart.

Measured against the extent of human habitation on the Creuddyn peninsula - 12,000 years since the first cave dwellers took up residence - this flow of publicity may seem like a scratching of surfaces. Here we have represented every stage of social evolution from Old Stone Age to electronic modernity: a concentrated version of the human saga. So much is yet to be revealed.

St Tudno would want to walk the shingle bar, now an impressive esplanade, between the two headlands he knew so well.

Route 5

Llandudno pier entrance - Little Orme - Penrhyn Old Hall: 6.2km, 3.9ml.

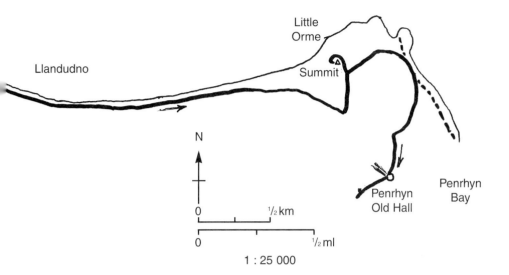

From the eastern end of the esplanade (2.4km, 1.5ml) continue through Craigside to a critch-cratch (2.9km, 1.8ml) at the side of the road.

Nearby is the site where, in 1907, a metal-strapped wooden box was found some 30 inches down into scree, containing about 500 Roman coins. Robert Barnsdale, a coin specialist, has established that these were brasses from the period 287- 293 when Mausaeus Carausius, who was commander of the Roman British fleet, seized power and ruled as Emperor of Britain and northern Gaul.

What crisis had compelled the gathering and burying of this hoard? With the empire already in decline it was a time of uncertainty. Carausius was murdered by one of his officers, Allectus, who set himself up as Emperor of Britain. He ruled until the year 296 when he was himself killed.

*   *   *

Up on the Little Orme is a fork in the path (3.2km, 2.0ml). Turn left from the fork and climb to the summit (3.4km, 2.3ml; elevation: 141m, 463ft).

Looking south-eastward beyond the settlements of Penrhyn Bay and across the delta of the Afon Ganol, once an outlet of the Conwy to the sea, Llandrillo church marks the headquarters of another Dark Age Saint. St Trillo founded his cell here, near the sheltering presence of Bryn Euryn, an old fortress hill where Maelgwn, or his vassals, could observe this developing Llan.

Northward from the summit are the sheer cliffs of Creigiau Rhiwledyn, the Little Orme's natural battlements, which may have been a factor in the siting here of a conspiracy related to the fate of nations. In 1536 the English government began the Reformation which would result in independence from the power of the Roman Church. By 1558, Protestantism was the state religion and Catholicism treasonable.

A counter-revolution gathered which included preparing Welsh-language texts, having them printed in Italy and smuggled into Wales. In 1580 a secret conference of priests agreed to establish clandestine printing presses in Britain.

The owner of Penrhyn Hall, Robert Pugh, was a sympathiser. He agreed to the siting of a clandestine press on his land - the first printing press in Wales - in a cliff cave here on the Little Orme at Rhiwledyn. The first tract was dated 1585. In 1587 the chief printer was arrested and subsequently executed. The government undertook a searching review of implications.

It was known that an armada was gathering in Spain. Its purpose was the conquest of Britain and restoration of Papal authority. In a struggle for survival, the response in Wales to invading forces could be vital.

An unexpected development followed. The government decided to authorise publication of William Morgan's Welsh translation of the Bible. Printing facilities were offered via the Royal Printer.

Published in the year the Spanish Armada sailed - 1588 - the Welsh Bible is generally acknowledged to be the most significant factor in the survival and continuation of the language.

*   *   *

Continue north-eastward round the headland above impressive seascape views, or return to the fork (3.2km) and follow the track up to a turning right (4.0km, 2.5ml).

Descend a zig-zag to a critch-cratch (4.2km), and an incline, to a right turn southward near the cliff edge, passing a broad shelf which was the centre of a quarrying industry for almost 50 years to 1931.

A path veers south-eastward down to the coast, along the shoreline by Colwyn Bay and on into Old Colwyn.

Pass through a critch-cratch (5.3km) and on to the main road (5.9km, 3.7ml).

Near here, in 1873, a hoard of about 5,000 Roman coins was unearthed two feet down in a single-handled, earthenware pot. Robert Barnsdale reports the coins were mostly brasses from the 2nd and 3rd centuries. Some 3,000 of them were minted in Britain, the remainder being of Gaulish origin. Generally, the coins were from the period 293 - 337.

What emergency produced this hideaway hoard? Probably an even more tense situation than that which caused the smaller hoard to be buried near the base of the Little Orme. The empire had entered its final century of decline. Britain was invaded from the south and east by imperial forces desperate to put down the local warlord usurper, Allectus. In the north, Scottish rebels were on the move preparing a powerful push that would eventually crash through Hadrian's Wall, while Irish incursion into Wales was underway.

*   *   *

Approach now the centre of an estate whose lands extended across Penrhyn Bay, and where the host nurtured a cell of Catholic resistance to the Protestant Reformation in the 16th century.

That was as recently as a little more than four centuries ago. Take the mind back a thousand years and we are at the time of the Dark Age Prince. All this to mull over in the welcoming atmosphere of Penrhyn Old Hall (6.2km, 3.9ml).

Route 6

Penrhyn Old Hall - Llanrhos Church - Castle of the Dark Age Prince,
Deganwy: 5.0km, 3.1ml.

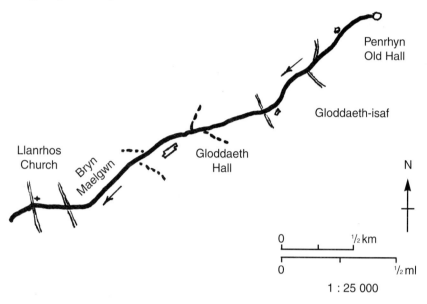

From the Old Hall continue SW and S along a track to a village road
(0.5km), veer right (0.6km) onto a path, then left past Gloddaeth-isaf
(0.8km) - the lower Gloddaeth - to a farm road (1.0km).

Leaving the roadside stile bear 258 degrees to a critch-cratch in the
corner of the field adjacent to Gloddaeth Hall (1.5km).

Here was luxuriant woodland, traces of which have survived 1500
years. The main hunting lodge was to the south at Bodyscallen, a resort
of Maelgwn's father, Caswallon, where the Dark Age Prince would have
spent much of his leisure time when the kingdom was relatively secure.
It was a good place for hatching plots. When a murder was necessary the
victim's remains could be easily disposed of. The hunting of wild boar
and the demise of an inconvenient opponent could be attended to in
much the same way. Anything could be concealed beneath centuries of
undergrowth.

The Normans were quick to spot advantage in a location. By 1584,
a millennium after Maelgwn, an estate house stood here at Gloddaeth. It
evolved through centuries to what may be seen today.

Continue along the path past the house to the front drive (1.8km)
and on to a critch-cratch (2.2km, 1.4ml). We are now crossing the
southern slope of Bryn Maelgwn - Maelgwn's Hill. It remains thickly

wooded, with an impenetrable ambience, enveloping the body of the Prince in an everlasting hiding place, legend relates, so no-one can wantonly wreak vengeance for his evil deeds.

Probe as we might on Bryn Maelgwn, another place a short distance to the west has a stronger claim on the Prince's remains.

Cross the road to a critch-cratch and continue westward across a field to Llanrhos Parish Church (3.0km, 1.9ml).

Maelgwn is credited with having founded this distinguished place of worship in his repentance period, under the influence of the mythical bard, Taliesin.

Taliesin nurtured no illusions about the Prince. Believing his crimes would be avenged, he set down a gruesome prophecy.

> Fe ddaw pryf rhyfedd
> O Forfa Rhianedd
> I ddial anwiredd
> Ar Faelgwn Gwynedd;
> A'i flew a'i ddannedd,
> A'i lygaid yn euredd,
> A hyn a wna ddiwedd
> Ar Faelgwn Gwynedd.

> A strange insect will come
> From Morfa Rhianedd
> To avenge the crimes
> Of Maelgwn Gwynedd;
> And its hair and teeth,
> And its golden eyes,
> And it's this that will bring an end
> To Maelgwn Gwynedd.

It is alleged The Prince came to this church to die after being infected by a plague that had arisen from the bodies of the dead he had slaughtered. One choice of date for his death - by G A Humphreys - is the year 547. Another - by W Bezant Lowe - is the year 560 - "of the Yellow Plague which lasted from 557 to 562."

Approach the Dark Age Prince's court through Llanrhos village to the boundary of The Vardre and castle entrance.

Climb the path to the summit of the principal motte (5.0km, 3. 1ml).

Look westward towards the Isle of Man. It is said the Prince annexed that island in the year 517, after slaughtering Scots who had occupied it.

* * *

The Llandudno Circuit

The Rock of Conwy to The Rock of Conwy
41km   26ml

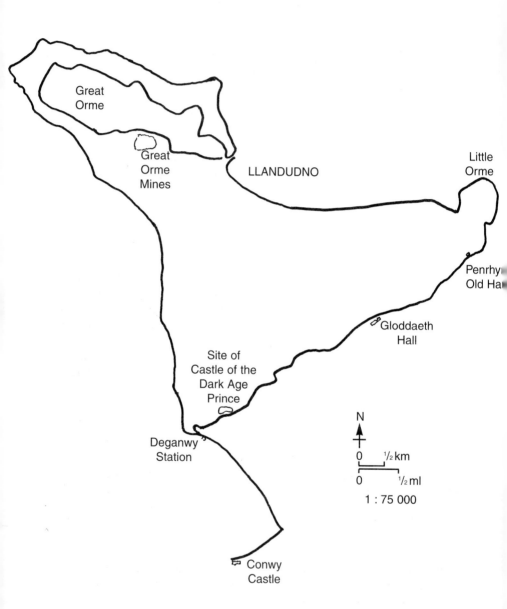

Great
Orme

Great
Orme
Mines

LLANDUDNO

Little
Orme

Penrhy
Old Ha

Gloddaeth
Hall

Site of
Castle of the
Dark Age
Prince

Deganwy
Station

N

0   ¹/₂ km
0   ¹/₂ ml
1 : 75 000

Conwy
Castle

Crossing the estuary by bridge one may reflect on those who once held power here - the ferrymen. How one would love to hear their ribald language while having the fate of travellers in their hands!

From the centre of the bridge the view north-west funnels out onto the site of ancient forests, now submerged beneath the sea that has been rising steadily for thousands of years.

Turn left off the bridge to Deganwy Quay and train station, and left again over the railway line onto the coastal path.

In the years from about 1000 to 1500, monks settled in most profoundly peaceful places that were conducive to reflection and meditation. They built their accommodation and lived in self-sufficiency. The ruin of Gogarth Abbey - regarded as a palace in possession of the Bishops of Bangor as well as a monastery under the abbots of Conwy is a monument to the monks' endeavours.

Seascape views change with every step round the Great Orme, passing the Orme's Head and lighthouse to the ancient copper smelting site at Pen-trwyn headland.

If the Circuit is to be done in two or three stages, the pier entrance would be a suitable place to break: 16.5km, 10.3 miles.

*   *   *

From the pier entrance veer left and left again, passing the Bronze Age lookout and fort, Pen y Dinas. Beyond the Ski Lodge and Pink Farm are some of the springs to which Llandudno owed its primary existence: first to the Bronze Age mining communities, then to the sixth-century crusader-founder, St Tudno.

From St Tudno's Church the route around the wall leads to the site of the incredible Bronze Age copper mines that sustained ancient communities for about 1,260 years.

Nearby is a Stone Age monument, aged perhaps 5,000 years.

On returning to the pier entrance the distance is: 25km, 15.6 ml.

*   *   *

Continue from the western end of the esplanade to the base of the Little Orme. Why did Roman Britons choose this site to bury hoards of coins? Leaving the critch-cratch by the roadside continue up to the Little Orme summit, down and around the headland and southward across the road to Penrhyn Old Hall.

Along tracks and pathways past Gloddaeth Hall continue to Llanrhos Church. Pause to consider why this particular site was chosen to locate the church. Just beyond a critch-cratch note the position of a well. Spring water again, the discovery St Tudno made up on the Great Orme.

Through the village to the site where the Dark Age Prince ruled Gwynedd from his castle over 700 years before a castle was raised on The Rock of Conwy. Total distance: 41km, 26ml.

Bibliography

Atkinson, David: Nant y Gamar, 1996
                            Guidebooks To Llandudno, 1998
                            A Bibliography Of Llandudno, 2001

Bannerman, Nigel: Bronze Age Coast Project, 1998

Bannerman, Diane and Nigel: The Great Orme Explained, 2000

Bezant Lowe, W: The Heart Of North Wales, 1912

Breverton, T D: The Book Of Welsh Saint, 2000

Dibble, Kenneth: Nant y Gamar, 1990
                            Rhiwledyn and The Little Orme, 1995

Draper, Christopher: Walks From Llandudno, 1999

Great Orme Exploration Society Newsletters, 1988-98

Great Orme Mines: Discover The Amazing
                            Great Orme Copper Mines, 1998

Gwynedd Archeological Trust: Pentrwyn Metal Working Site Great Orme,
                            1999

Humphries, G A: Deganwy Castle, 1910

Parry, Tom: Llys Helig, 1996

Roberts, Askew: Gossiping Guide To Wales, 1880

Rowlands, E D: Dyffryn Conwy a'r Creuddyn, 1947

Watkins, David: Deg 0 Dywysogion, 1963

Wicklen, S I: Cave Printers Of The Little Orme

WALK in the Realm of the Dark Age Prince
LLANDUDNO

Acknowledgements

With grateful thanks to:

DAVID ATKINSON: for advice, materials, consultations,
                         introductions, script readings

NIGEL BANNERMAN: for consultation and map origination
marine archeologist   of the Conwy estuary
                         for permission to print photographs of
                         Stone Age and Bronze Age tools in
                         personal possession

ROBERT BARNSDALE: for advice on Roman coin hoards

DAVID CHAPMAN: for portrait of the Dark Age Prince

DAVE O'SHEA   for photography

GREAT ORME MINES LTD   for permission to print photographs taken
                         at the mine

LLANDUDNO LIBRARY

LLANDUDNO MUSEUM

MUSEUM OF LONDON   for print of Bronze Age boat

Special thanks to:

ALWENA   as always

The WALK Snowdonia Series

by the same author

ISBN

Walk in the beautiful Conwy Valley	1 -872050-00-X
Walk in magnificent Snowdonia	1-872050-02-6

Walk Snowdonia   1-872050-03-4
         ancient trackways
         Roman roads
         packhorse trails

Walk in the romantic Vale of Ffestiniog   1-872050-04-2
           Porthmadog
             Cricieth

Walk Snowdonia Peaks   1-872050-05-0

All are available through bookshops and other bookseller outlets

The WALK Snowdonia Series

forthcoming title

WALK in the beautiful Conwy Valley

7th edition

enlarged .. revised

ISBN: 1-872050-07-7

Focus Publications Ltd
Tel: 01789 298948   Fax: 01789 294845
E-mail: maddern@focusproductions.co.uk